The Shaping of the Continents

by Peggy Bresnick Kendler

PEARSON

Scott
Foresman

Editorial Offices: Glenview, Illinois • Parsippany, New Jersey • New York, New York
Sales Offices: Needham, Massachusetts • Duluth, Georgia • Glenview, Illinois
Coppell, Texas • Ontario, California • Mesa, Arizona

Illustrations Susan J. Carlson

Photographs

Every effort has been made to secure permission and provide appropriate credit for photographic material. The publisher deeply regrets any omission and pledges to correct errors called to its attention in subsequent editions.

Unless otherwise acknowledged, all photographs are the property of Pearson Education, Inc.

Cover DK Images; **1** ©Royalty-Free/Corbis; **3** ©Royalty-Free/Corbis; **6** SZ Photo/ Knorr + Hirth/DIZ Muenchen GmbH, Sueddeutsche Zeitung Photo/Alamy Images; **12** DK Images; **14** Daniel Prudek/Fotolia; **15** GOL/Fotolia; **16** Nguyen/MCT/NewsCom; **17** Dreamframer/Shutterstock; **21** ©Royalty-Free/Corbis.

ISBN: 0-328-13573-9

16   16

The Continents Are Always Moving

The planet Earth, as we know it today, consists of seven continents separated by the world's oceans. Scientists believe this was not always the case. Rather, evidence suggests that hundreds of millions of years ago Earth's continents were in different locations and possibly even joined together.

If you look at the shapes of the continents as they are today, they look like puzzle pieces. If you moved them closer, they could almost fit together. The eastern coast of South America would fit together with the western coast of Africa, for instance.

Also, fossils of tropical plants that only grow in warm climates have been found in Antarctica, suggesting that the continent may have once been in a warmer place.

Pangaea

According to one model, Earth's continents have gone through big changes in the last 225 million years.

About 225 million years ago, Earth's surface had a single land mass. The one enormous **supercontinent** was called Pangaea, which means "all lands" in Greek. It included all the land from North America, South America, Africa, Europe, Asia, Australia, and Antarctica. A single sea called Panthalassa surrounded Pangaea.

Then, in the 25 million years that followed, Earth's crust shifted and began to tear the supercontinent apart. Within 75 million years Pangaea had broken into two distinct landmasses called Laurasia and Gondwanaland. Laurasia was located in the northern hemisphere and Gondwanaland in the southern hemisphere.

225 million years ago
Pangaea

By 60 million years ago, Laurasia and Gondwanaland had broken into the seven continents that we see today. Laurasia split into North America, Europe, and Asia. Gondwanaland split into South America, Africa, Australia, and Antarctica. As the continents separated, Earth's one great ocean also became separated into smaller oceans: the Pacific Ocean, which separates the west coast of North America and eastern Asia; the Atlantic Ocean, which sits between eastern North America and the western coasts of Africa and Europe; and the Indian Ocean, which is between southern Asia and northern Australia.

While scientists have been able to show that the continents are still shifting and moving today, they are still learning why and how the process works. The theory devoted to explaining this question is called continental drift.

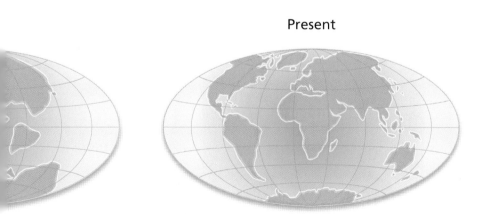

Present

Continental Drift Theory

Alfred Wegener, a German meteorologist, first suggested the theory of continental drift in 1912. Wegener's hypothesis that continents move around Earth's surface was based on his observation that the coasts of South America and Africa seemed to fit together. These matching coastlines also contained the same plant and animal **fossils,** as well as similar rock and land formations.

When first posed, Wegener's theory was considered **unconventional.** In fact, some of his fellow scientists offered only the harshest criticism of it. One scientist called it "footloose." Another called it "rot." Still another complained that if Wegener's hypothesis were to gain acceptance, scientists would have to "forget everything we have learned in the last 70 years and start all over again." Most geologists of the time thought that Earth's landmasses were static—they stayed put and did not move at all.

Alfred Wegener

6

One problem with Wegener's theory was that it didn't explain just how the continents moved. Wegener thought that the continents might be moving through Earth's crust, just as an icebreaker might move through a sheet of ice. However, no one could figure out what force on Earth was powerful enough to move such large landmasses at all, much less over such great distances.

While many scientists of the time rejected Wegener's theory, some others saw merit in it. Wegener spent the rest of his life trying to support his theory. After Wegener died in 1930, the scientists who had been intrigued by his ideas continued to seek an answer to the question of what could cause continents to move. However, it looked as if Wegener's theory of continental drift would become a footnote in the study of geology.

Then, in the 1950s, scientists studying the ocean floor began to make discoveries that brought new attention to Wegener's theory. They observed that the floor of the Atlantic Ocean was spreading out from a ridge of undersea mountains and volcanoes. That spreading made the ocean wider and moved the continents on either side of it farther and farther apart.

Scientists developed a new theory to explain these new findings and to solve Wegener's problem about what force was strong enough to move whole continents. This theory is called plate tectonics.

Plate Tectonics

According to the theory of plate tectonics, continents do not simply drift over Earth's surface, or through Earth's crust, as Wegener suggested, but are pushed and pulled by forces within Earth. Before you can understand plate tectonics, though, you have to know what Earth is made of.

Earth is made of layers: the crust, the mantle, and the core. Each layer has its own properties. The surface is called the crust. The crust can be many miles thick, but is brittle and can break easily. Underneath the crust lies the mantle. The mantle is made of very hot, **plastic** rock that flows and bends like a really thick liquid. At the center of Earth is the core. The core is made mostly of iron and has two parts. The outer core is molten iron. The inner core is solid and very hot—as hot as the surface of the sun. The pressure of the outer core keeps the inner core solid.

The plate tectonics theory holds that Earth's crust is made up of many large plates. These plates are made of rock and float on the surface of the mantle. They can be as thin as 9 miles or as thick as 124 miles and can be thousands of miles across. These plates are called tectonic plates.

Scientists think that tectonic plates probably have been moving over Earth's surface for billions of years, coming together and separating, over and over again. This cycle is called the Wilson cycle and is named after John Tuzo Wilson, the Canadian scientist who first developed this theory.

Scientists think that the formation of the continents and all movements within Earth, including earthquakes and volcanoes, are caused by the movement of these plates.

Major Tectonic Plates

- **A** Pacific Plate
- **B** North American Plate
- **C** Cocos Plate
- **D** Nazca Plate
- **E** South American Plate
- **F** African Plate
- **G** Eurasian Plate
- **H** Indian Plate
- **I** Australian Plate
- **J** Antarctic Plate

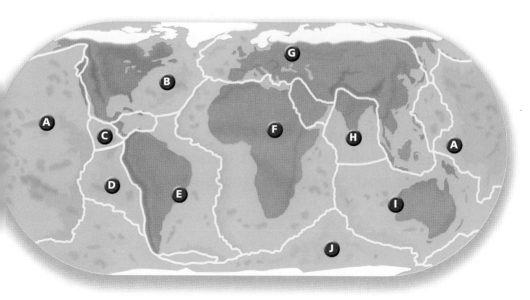

Types of Plate Motion

Tectonic plates move in many different ways, although what causes the plates to move is still a mystery. The most popular explanation is the convection theory.

Convection is the process where heat rises and cool air falls. Think of how air rises in a room and then is pushed sideways as it reaches the ceiling. Currents lower in the mantle, closer to the outer core, are hotter than those near the crust. According to this theory, the movement of hotter and cooler layers of mantle causes the plates floating along the surface of the mantle to move. Think of the way ocean currents can carry ships along.

Scientists have observed that tectonic plates move in three different ways. They can move toward each other, move away from each other, or slide by each other. Each motion creates a different effect. For example, when two plates move apart, or **diverge,** molten rock from within the mantle spews forth, creating new ocean floor.

Most of the boundaries between plates are hidden beneath the oceans, so we can't see them. Most of Earth's volcanic activity and earthquakes happen along these boundaries. Today, the ocean's plate boundaries are mapped from outer space. Satellites high above Earth's surface are able to measure both the size and location of plates.

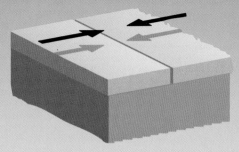

Convergent plate movement is when two plates move toward each other. They can crash or one can slide beneath the other.

Divergent plate movement is when two plates move away from each other.

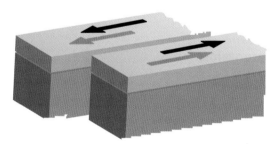

Sliding plate movement is when two plates slide by each other at a fracture boundary.

New Land, Recycled Land

The sea-floor spreading that scientists observed at the mid-ocean ridge in the Atlantic Ocean is an example of tectonic plates that are diverging. It is also a clue as to how the plates move. Look at the diagram below.

At spreading centers, or divergent plate boundaries, new land is being made. At the plate boundary, **magma** rises from deep within the mantle to the surface of Earth's crust. As convection currents pull the plates in different directions, magma rises to fill the space between the plates. However, the force of the rising magma may also be pushing the plates apart as it rises to the surface. When the magma hits the surface, it becomes lava. The ocean water cools the lava, which, in turn, hardens to become new sea floor.

As the sea floor spreads, it pushes the tectonic plates away from the spreading center, moving the plates and the landmasses that ride on them away from the spreading center as well.

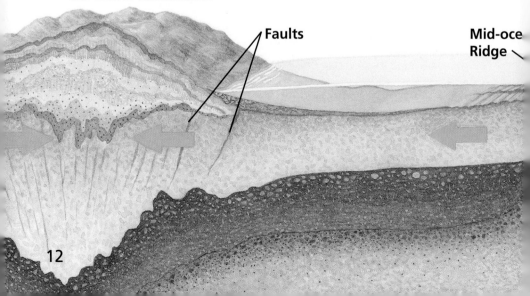

Colliding plates can create mountains.

Faults

Mid-oce Ridge

If new land is being created at the mid-ocean ridges, what happens to the land on the other side of the plate? It meets other plates to form a convergent plate boundary. The way the plates meet, or **converge,** depends on whether the land at the plate boundary is ocean floor or part of a landmass such as a continent.

The land that makes up the ocean floor is denser than the land that makes up a continental landmass. When an ocean-floor boundary meets a landmass, the denser ocean floor will always slide under the less-dense landmass and sink back into the mantle. This process is called **subduction.** Eventually, over many millions of years, the subducted material will reach another mid-ocean ridge and rise again to become sea floor. In this way, the rock that makes up Earth's crust is recycled.

The process of subduction can trigger deep earthquakes. Also, the friction caused as one plate plunges beneath the other melts some of the rocks, producing magma. This magma then forces its way to the surface of the landmass. When it breaks through, it forms a volcano. Whole ranges of volcanic mountains can form along subduction zones. The Andes mountain range in South America is one example.

Sea Floor Spreading

Subduction Zone

Trench

Subduction can form volcanoes.

Magma

13

Magma

When Plates Collide

You just read about what happens when the denser rock of an ocean floor plate boundary meets the less-dense rock of a landmass. What happens when the two plate boundaries are both the edges of landmasses? Since neither plate will subduct, the two plates crash into each other. The land on the edges of the convergent plate boundaries folds and crumples. Sometimes huge chunks of bedrock—the foundation rock of the continent—are pushed over or under other pieces of bedrock. This type of plate collision builds mountain ranges.

The Himalaya Mountains in Asia are an example of this process. Many millions of years ago, what is now India was a separate continent, divided from Asia by an ocean called the Tethys Sea. Around 60 million years ago, the Indian Plate began colliding with the Asian Plate. Within 40 million years, the Tethys Sea had completely closed due to this collision. The force of the collision also pushed up the lofty Himalaya Mountains, which boast the highest mountains on Earth. The collision is still occurring, and the Himalayas, including Mount Everest, continue to rise.

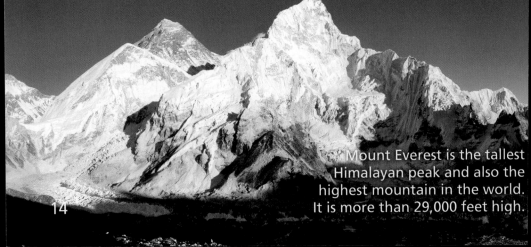

Mount Everest is the tallest Himalayan peak and also the highest mountain in the world. It is more than 29,000 feet high.

Plate collisions may explain the towering Himalayas, but what about a rounded, rolling mountain range such as the Appalachians? That question is harder to answer because the Appalachian Mountains are extremely ancient.

Scientists think that the Appalachians might have been formed when ancient landmasses collided. This collision may have been part of the continental drift that formed the supercontinent of Pangaea. If this is the case, the Appalachians began to form in much the same way as the Himalayas. In fact, they may once have been as high or higher than the Himalayas are today.

Hundreds of millions of years have passed since then, and the Appalachians have been eroded by wind, water, and weather—several times, in fact. Geologic forces have caused the land of these mountains to uplift, or rise in elevation more than once through the ages. After each uplift, more erosion has occurred.

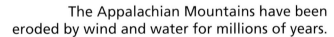

The Appalachian Mountains have been eroded by wind and water for millions of years.

A Plate-Boundary Fault Line

Some tectonic plates meet, but they neither subduct nor collide. Instead, they slide along beside each other. These boundaries are called fracture boundaries. The place where the plates meet forms a fault—a crack or fracture in Earth's surface. You can see how a fracture boundary moves by observing the San Andreas Fault.

The San Andreas Fault is where the Pacific Plate and the North American Plate meet. It is around 800 miles long and runs through parts of western Mexico north through western California. The Pacific Plate is moving northwest, while the North American Plate is moving southeast. In some places along the fault, this movement is slow and rather steady. At other places, however, the plates can get stuck. Strain builds up—sometimes for many years—and eventually the pressure is too much. The stuck portion of the fault gives way and the plates move. This movement produces an earthquake. Depending on the distance the plates move and the energy released, such an earthquake can be very dangerous to lives and property.

Los Angeles

Palm Springs

San Andreas fault

NORTH AMERICAN PLATE

Az.

Calif.

Pacific Ocean

Salton Trough

Salton Sea

San Diego

Imperial fault

PACIFIC PLATE

MEX.

Cerro Prieto fault

Ensenada

50 miles
50 km

Source: ESRI
Graphic: Khang Nguyen,
Los Angeles Times   © 2011 MCT

Gulf of Calif.

If you want to see how far the San Andreas Fault has moved in the last 20 million years or so, visit Pinnacles National Monument southeast of Salinas, California. It is on the west side of the San Andreas Fault. The Pinnacles are dramatic, unusual rock formations—what is left of part of the Neenah Volcano.

Geologists believe the Neenah Volcano last erupted around 23 million years ago. However, the Pinnacles are only part of what is left of the volcano. The other part of the volcano lies nearly 200 miles southeast of the Pinnacles, near the city of Lancaster, California! This part of the Neenah Volcano lies on the east side of the San Andreas Fault. The San Andreas Fault split the volcano, and fault movement carried the Pinnacles north to their present location.

The northern California city of San Francisco lies on the North American Plate, just east of the San Andreas Fault. The city of Los Angeles, in southern California, lies west of the San Andreas Fault. If these cities continue to exist for millions of years, one day they may be neighbors!

The Pinnacles were formed from an ancient volcano.

The Ring of Fire

How do the movements of tectonic plates and continents affect us today? Throughout most of human history, people did not understand what caused the land beneath their feet to shake or volcanoes to spew ash and lava over their cities and farms. Today, we know that plate movements form many of Earth's volcanoes and cause most earthquakes. The study of plate tectonics can help scientists understand these forces so that one day they may be able to predict volcanic eruptions and earthquakes more exactly.

For example, scientists are giving much study to a string of volcanoes and faults that encircle the landmasses surrounding the Pacific Ocean. They call this the "Ring of Fire." Many of Earth's active volcanoes are located along the Ring of Fire. Many earthquakes occur along the Ring of Fire every year. Look at the map of the Ring of Fire below, and then look at the map of tectonic plates on page 9. Notice how the boundaries of the Pacific Plate match up to the Ring of Fire.

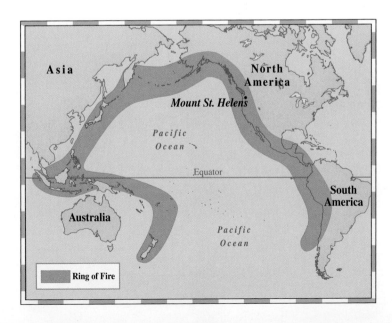

By observing the volcanoes of the Ring of Fire, scientists now know that certain signs can signal that an eruption is near. Let's look at what scientists observed at Mount St. Helens, a volcano that is part of the Cascade Mountain Range in Oregon.

For most of the 1900s, Mount St. Helens was renowned for its beauty. It was a perfect snow-capped peak that attracted hikers and sightseers. People knew it was a volcano, but it hadn't erupted in a long time. Who knew when or if it would erupt again?

Then, in March, 1980, the volcano began rumbling. Earthquakes, caused by the movement of magma deep beneath the mountain, shook the area. Blasts of steam erupted from the mountain. A bulge formed on the north side of the mountain—magma was forcing its way to the surface.

Scientists predicted that an eruption would occur very soon. They warned people to stay away from the mountain, although some people did not pay attention. Then, on May 18, 1980, Mount St. Helens erupted, sending ash and rock hurling miles into the sky and causing an enormous avalanche that traveled fifteen miles in ten minutes.

Today, new forests are replacing those that were blasted away by the eruption or buried by the avalanche. People come to see the mountain and hike on or near it, when they are allowed to. Scientists monitor the mountain closely, though, because they are sure it will erupt again one day.

Continental Movement in the Future

Tectonic plates are always moving. Yet, we are not likely to see much of a difference in our planet's appearance during our lifetimes. This is because plates move at a very, very slow rate.

Today's scientists use computer models to predict what the future will bring for Earth's features. Scientists believe that the Atlantic Ocean will continue to expand and the Pacific Ocean will likely shrink in size. The Mediterranean Sea will disappear entirely, and the continent of Africa will be connected to Europe. In the future, India will continue pushing into the southern part of Asia. This will make the Himalaya Mountains even higher than they are today. Western California will slide northward toward Alaska. Australia will move northward as well. Eventually, it will collide with Asia. In fact, one day, maybe 250 million years from now, Earth may once again have only one continent—a supercontinent to rival Pangaea.

Of course, all of these changes will not happen overnight. In fact, these dramatic changes to Earth's surface are most likely going to take tens or even hundreds of millions of years to occur.

In the meantime, we can expect the massive peaks in the Himalayas to grow just a little bit taller each year. We can expect to see small changes in landforms all around the world. Our planet will continue to be shaped by earthquakes and volcanic eruptions.

Mountains created by plates that have collided with each other will continue to grow in height. The Himalayas are now growing slightly taller each year.

Now Try This

Plate Movement

When tectonic plates drift across the surface of Earth, forces deep inside our planet move them. Today, you are going to be the force that moves the plates.

In this activity, you'll have the opportunity to see, firsthand, how the movement of plates alters Earth's landmasses and makes changes in the landscape.

You will need a slab of modeling clay for this activity. First, divide the clay into two pieces that are about the same size. Flatten each piece of clay with your hands or roll it out with a rolling pin. When you have two pieces of clay that are about the thickness of a pancake, you are ready to begin.

Each piece of flattened modeling clay represents one tectonic plate. You will push the clay together in two different ways.

1. To demonstrate how two plates collide, do this: While keeping one of the clay pieces on a table or other flat surface, gently push the second piece into the one on the table.

   What happens to each piece of clay? Do they remain flat? Do they change in some specific way? Record your observations on a piece of paper.

2. To demonstrate subduction, when one plate slides underneath another plate, do this: Again, roll out or flatten both pieces of clay. Lift each piece to make sure it sits loosely on a table or other flat surface. Gently slide the two pieces together, allowing one piece of clay to slide partially underneath the other.

   What happens to each piece of clay? Do they change in any way after one has slid underneath the other? Record your findings.

3. Now look at your notes. How are these plate movements different? How are they similar? Imagine these pieces of clay as actual tectonic plates and explain how a continent might be altered in each kind of plate movement. Share your observations with a classmate, if possible.

Glossary

converge *v.* come together.

diverge *v.* to split apart from.

fossils *n.* remains of plants or animals that lived in the past, preserved as rock.

magma *n.* molten rock beneath the Earth's surface.

plastic *adj.* easily molded or shaped.

subduction *n.* the process of one tectonic plate sliding underneath another tectonic plate.

supercontinent *n.* a mass of land with more than one continent.

unconventional *adj.* not conforming to accepted rules or standards.